Original title:
Plum Perfection

Copyright © 2025 Creative Arts Management OÜ
All rights reserved.

Author: Maxwell Donovan
ISBN HARDBACK: 978-1-80586-391-5
ISBN PAPERBACK: 978-1-80586-863-7

Lush Ambrosia

In a garden, round and deep,
The fruits all whisper, 'Come and leap!'
Bouncing high on branches tight,
Giggles rise with every bite.

A purple glob, a joyful sight,
It wiggles, giggles, with delight.
Juicy treasure drips and drops,
Planting smiles like candy shops.

Playground of Nature

Swinging high, the branches sway,
Fruit fighters dance in bright array.
Tossing berries, oh what fun,
Watch them splat, we're on the run!

A squirrel joins the playful spree,
Nibbles snacks and climbs a tree.
Belly laughs, a burst of cheer,
Nature's circus, always near.

Savoring Seasons

Springtime sings in colors bold,
With giggles wrapped in petals' fold.
Late summer's tease, a fruity fling,
Who knew they'd make us laugh and sing?

Autumn's jokes roll off the vine,
As laughter swells like aged fine wine.
Winter's chill can't dim the fun,
With frosty treats in the sun.

Fruits of Whimsy

A bouncing berry with a flair,
Makes the blues fade without a care.
In the jester's crown, it reigns,
Playing pranks with sticky stains.

Munching merrily, the fruit brigade,
Chasing flavors that never fade.
In every bite, a giggle found,
With fruity frolics all around.

The Harvest's Kiss

In the orchard, fruits collide,
A dance of flavors, side by side.
Bouncing baskets, laughter loud,
Every drop sung by the crowd.

With sticky hands and grin so wide,
We test the ripe ones, can't abide.
One's too sour, another sweet,
Taste buds chaotically compete!

A giggle bursts with every bite,
Who knew food could be so bright?
When all is said and done, oh snap!
Will this fashion be a mishap?

We toast our hats in silly cheers,
To juicy bombs that bring us tears.
In this moment, joy runs free,
Who knew harvests could be glee?

Savoring Joy's Essence

In the kitchen, chaos reigns,
Sweet medley slips from our veins.
Jars are clinking, lids are tight,
Can we brew a tasty sight?

A recipe, oh what a feat,
Measured laughs, can't feel my feet.
Mixing wild, it's all a race,
Splatters land with shiny grace!

Taste testing, laughter brews,
With every bite, we pay our dues.
One too tart? Oh, what a shame!
We'll just add more silly game!

In the end, we cheer so loud,
Who knew mishaps drew a crowd?
With flavors spun from joy untold,
We dance in sweetness, brave and bold!

Sweet Aroma of Eden

In a garden of velvet, they twirl,
With cheeks like ripe fruit in a whirl.
The bees buzz a tune, all a-flutter,
While squirrels plot ways to steal their butter.

Sun-drenched and juicy, with glee they boast,
"Why'd you pick me? I'm not your host!"
But their smiles are wide, and they know the deal,
A laugh and a bite, it's their fruity appeal.

The Art of Ripeness

A rogue on a branch, in a dashing hue,
Said, "I'm not soft! Just waiting for you!"
The art of being ripe takes skill, you see,
Like dodging the nectar-thief, who's full of glee.

With each passing day, they puff up with pride,
As they wink at the passing ants that glide.
"Nice try, little friend! You must understand,
It takes finesse to be in high demand!"

Richness in Simplicity

A fruit in the bowl, so round and so bold,
Whispers, "I'm simple yet worth more than gold!"
With just a soft squeeze, it laughs with delight,
"No need for fanfare, I'm perfect, just right!"

They gather in groups, all cozy and neat,
Planning their heist with a sneaky little beat.
"Who'll be the first to roll down the stairs?
Let's turn this dull kitchen into fruit fairs!"

Bounty of the Earth

Bathed in sunlight, they giggle with glee,
"We're the bounty, joyful as can be!"
With laughter and juice, they conquer the plate,
In a world full of snacks, they are just first-rate!

Under the tree, they plot and conspire,
Sharing their tales, fueling the fire.
"Who knew being fruit could be so grand?
Join us on this weird, wobbly land!"

The Harvest of Whimsy

In the orchard, fruits are round,
The squirrels dance, so unbound.
Jars of jam, a sticky mess,
Who knew harvest could caress?

Giggling beans and fruity cheer,
Each bite brings a joyful sneer.
We've dropped the basket, what a sight,
A pie fight turned into delight!

Fragrant Whispers in the Breeze

A gentle breeze starts to tease,
With scents that float like swarming bees.
We sip our juice, oh what glee,
These fruits hang low, come dance with me!

Lemonade from nature's stash,
Watch out for that splat! Oh no, a crash!
Birds squawking jokes from tree to tree,
Nature's humor, come sip with me!

Orchard Secrets Unfold

Under leaves, a treasure hides,
Juicy secrets, nature bides.
Can you guess what's growing here?
A fruit so sweet, you'll shed a tear.

With aprons on, we hit the ground,
Who knew dirt could be so profound?
Twisting vines and giggly spills,
Laughter echoes with our thrills.

Nature's Juve Leaf

When life gives you greens, make a face,
Spin around with fruity grace.
Chasing unicorns through the grass,
Don't look back, let the good times amass!

The trees clapped with every cheer,
Bouncing around, we have no fear.
Nature's antics in the bright sun,
Join the fun, and let's all run!

Juicy Secrets Beneath Skin

There's a fruit that holds a surprise,
Unzip its skin, you'll find the prize.
Juice drips down, it's quite a scene,
Like a drama, sticky and green.

The neighbors peek, they want to share,
But they don't know, it's quite rare.
With one big bite, they get a taste,
Now all my secrets are laid to waste!

Abundant Sunset

In the orchard, a sunset shines,
With fruit that's blushing, in straight lines.
I wear a hat to catch the glow,
And dance around with a juicy flow.

The squirrels giggle, sipping juice,
While I consider if I should spruce.
But the best part of my sunny plight,
Is when they join in, what a sight!

Nature's Blush

Oh look at nature's rosy glow,
The fruit so round, it puts on a show.
It shines in sunlight, soft and sweet,
Like a comedian, can't stay discreet.

With every munch, I giggle loud,
This is the fruit that makes me proud.
I burst with laughter, juice on my chin,
A comedy act, let the fun begin!

Honeyed Aspirations

Dreaming big of honey drips,
With fruit so round, it plays its tricks.
I plant my wishes in garden rows,
Hoping for sweetness, and double grows.

Each fruit a dream, each bite a laugh,
Beneath its skin, a juicy half.
So as I pluck, my heart sings out,
Life is sweet, there's no doubt!

Rain-kissed Treasures

Raindrops dance on fruity cheeks,
Nature's children play hide and seek.
Splashes of color, oh what a sight,
Juicy gems glowing, pure delight.

Sipping nectar, like it's fine wine,
A fruity fiesta, feeling divine.
Who needs diamonds, or pearls so grand?
Just give me fruit from this bountiful land.

Orchard Dreams

In the orchard, dreams take flight,
Bouncing fruit, oh what a sight!
Twirling kids with glee abound,
Laughing, tumbling, on the ground.

Chasing shadows, giggles galore,
Who would've thought fruit could soar?
A fruit fight here, a splash over there,
Life's little joys thrown in the air.

Bursting with Flavor

Bursting berries, sweet and bright,
Wobbling softly, pure delight.
With every bite, a joyful cheer,
Flavors dancing, oh dear, oh dear!

Watch them wiggle, watch them jiggle,
Wobble and sway, never a riddle.
Fruitful laughter, like confetti rain,
In this tasty, fruity refrain.

The Sweet Succulence

Sinking teeth in, oh what a thrill,
Juices running, can't stop, won't spill.
Sticky fingers, messy face,
A flavor race, oh what a chase!

That sweet nectar, a golden spree,
Like candy apples, but best for me.
Every bite a jolly jest,
In this fruit world, I am blessed!

The Luster of Late Summer

In twilight's glow, they hang with pride,
Beneath the sun, they take a ride.
Bouncing round in grass so green,
Chubby cheeks, a funny scene.

With sticky hands, we make a mess,
A fruit fight leads to pure duress.
Laughter floats on summer air,
Spitting seeds without a care.

Grandma's pie, the talk of town,
But who can wear that fruity crown?
With every bite, we sing and dance,
Delightfully lost in our own romance.

So here's to summer, bright and bold,
An orchard tale, forever told.
With every laugh and juicy taste,
In silly hats, let's not waste haste.

Nectar's Secret

Hidden treasures up on high,
Are they sweet or just a lie?
Pull the branch, hear a thunk,
Just my luck, I hit a skunk.

Little critters gather round,
While I drop the juiciest found.
Their furry paws, so quick and sly,
Stealing moments as I sigh.

A honeyed nectar, fun and bold,
Each drop a story to be told.
But twist my tongue and take a drink,
And suddenly, I'm on the brink!

Oh sweet delight, so full of cheer,
I might just need another beer!
A sticky mess from head to toes,
In nectar's game, I'll take my blows.

Orchard Whispers

In the orchard, secrets flow,
With chuckles hiding down below.
Bouncing fruits with silly grins,
Giggles start where laughter begins.

A tree with branches all askew,
Sways and swirls, with friends anew.
Underneath, we plot and scheme,
For the juiciest summer dream.

Talking trees with faces bright,
Share the gossip, day and night.
If you listen close, you'll hear,
The cheeky tales that linger here.

So come and join this fruity fun,
A world of giggles 'neath the sun.
Harvest laughter, one by one,
In whispers sweet, our joy is spun.

Juicy Reminiscence

Remember when we hopped the fence?
In search of fruit, all made sense.
Chasing dreams on playful toes,
Hiding out from nosy crows.

We'd pluck them ripe, just like a pro,
Then laugh out loud, just letting go.
With juice on faces, all aglow,
Oh, the sweetness we'd bestow!

Those summer days, forever clear,
With every grin, we tasted cheer.
Adventures bold, we'd never hide,
Just fruity fun, a wild ride.

Now we gather, tell our tale,
With juicy laughs that never pale.
A trip down memory lane so bright,
Our friendship strong, a true delight.

Petals and Pits

Petals dancing in the breeze,
An unusual sight, if you please.
They pirouette with such grace,
Hiding pits in a cheeky place.

Watch your step, oh careful friend,
These little fruits can make you bend.
A tumble here, a giggle there,
Nature's jest—beyond compare!

Beneath the Boughs

Beneath the boughs where shadows lay,
A rogue fruit rolls and starts to play.
It wobbles, bounces, and takes flight,
A fruity prank — oh, what a sight!

Friends gather round, their laughter loud,
Chasing tangy thrills, feeling proud.
Who knew a fruit could cause such cheer,
With every bite, we cheer and jeer!

Evening's Crimson Glow

As evening falls, the sky ignites,
With crimson shades of tasty sights.
A fruit-filled feast that makes us grin,
Oh what a time, let the fun begin!

Sipping juice that dribbles wide,
Sticky fingers — can't hide our pride.
With every munch, a giggle flows,
In this glow, our laughter grows!

Gastronomic Euphoria

A plate adorned with shades so bright,
Each fruit a treasure, pure delight.
We snack away, a funny song,
Chortling loud as we munch along.

Friends make faces, bite and chew,
A comedy show with every hue.
Who thought this fruit could taste so grand?
In gastronomic bliss, we stand!

Sweet Temptations

In the orchard, fruit hangs low,
Beneath its skin, a secret glow.
A bite reveals the juicy treat,
Sweetness dances, can't be beat.

Chubby cheeks and sticky hands,
Gobbling fruit, it never lands.
A laugh erupts with every squirt,
Who knew that joy could come from dirt?

Little friends in a fruit-filled race,
Chasing laughter, oh what a chase!
Rolling down the grassy hill,
Who needs a plan? We've got the thrill!

With every pit, a story's told,
Of daring bites and fruits so bold.
So gather round, don't you delay,
Let's munch and giggle the day away!

Colors of Joy

Round and round the basket spins,
With shades that make our heads do spins.
Glistening skins of purple hue,
They whisper tales of summer's dew.

Gobble one and then another,
A juicy smile, oh brother, brother!
Dancing juice on tiny lips,
As laughter erupts in happy quips.

Two small hands reach for the prize,
With gleaming eyes, they strategize.
A burst of flavor, a happy song,
In this playful fruit, we belong.

Passed around, the bites we share,
Sticky fingers everywhere.
And as the sun begins to sink,
None can resist the fruits, I think!

Orchard's Lullaby

Underneath the tree, we play,
Where sleepy fruits hang out all day.
An afternoon of giggles blares,
As we toss and catch, with fruity flares.

A sleepy snack, with dreams so bright,
The juice runs wild, such pure delight.
With every bite, a tiny snore,
As laughter fades, who could want more?

Each little pit is a treasure found,
As mischief bounces all around.
Digging deep in the grassy bed,
The golden sun keeps overhead.

Snuggled in, we drift away,
As the orchard starts to sway.
In our dreams, the fruits will tease,
Whispering secrets on the breeze!

Exquisite Nectar

On the table, splashes of hue,
A banquet fit for me and you.
Sipping nectar, it tickles the tongue,
While silly songs keep us young.

A fruity feast that makes us grin,
With every splash, new fun begins.
Sticky syrup from cheek to cheek,
Laughter bubbles as we peek.

Tiny drips like little jewels,
In this garden of vibrant rules.
Bouncing from toast to bread,
Each bite a place where joy is spread.

So come and join this fruity spree,
Cut the fruit and dance with glee.
Let's toast to laughter, cheers all round,
In this nectar, happiness is found!

Nature's Sweet Serenade

In summer's heat, they dangle bright,
Like tiny gems, a fruity sight.
With cheeks so round, they bounce with glee,
They giggle softly, 'Come taste me!'

They wiggle on the branch and tease,
Like children playing in the breeze.
Juicy laughter, what a fun treat,
A dance of flavors, oh so sweet!

Birds chirp loud, they must agree,
These luscious orbs are pure jubilee.
With every bite, a silly grin,
A fruit-filled feast, let the fun begin!

So gather round, the harvest's grand,
A funny tale, let's make a stand.
Nature's gifts in playful delight,
A juicy joke to share tonight!

Garden of Pleasures

In my garden, round and true,
Bouncing fruits in every hue.
They slip and slide in a warm embrace,
Their playful charms fill every space.

Wobbling on the branches high,
They dare me with a cheeky sigh.
One took a leap — oh, what a sight!
Rolling down, it won the fight!

Juggling fruits, a circus show,
They bounce around, putting on a glow.
A splash of juice, a squishy mess,
Laughter bursts, no need to stress!

Gnomes in hats take breaks to snack,
They join the fruit, a fun-filled pack.
With every bite, a giggling cheer,
In this garden, joy's always near!

Whispers of the Flesh

Fruits are shy, they blush so red,
Hiding under leaves like dreams in bed.
Their sweet whispers float in the air,
'Come take a taste, if you dare!'

They play hide and seek amid the green,
With cheeky smiles, they gleam and preen.
Their juice is bold, a fruity jest,
A playful bite is always best!

Dancers on a plate, a funny crew,
Singing praises, 'Here, I'm for you!'
They split and burst with a fruity laugh,
In this shindig, they steal the half!

So grab a fork, dig in real deep,
With every bite, a giggle to keep.
Oh what a treat, don't clean your plate,
The laughter here can't wait to date!

A Symphony of Ripeness

The orchard's alive with a merry tune,
Fruits in harmony under the moon.
Plucking notes from branches high,
A juicy melody fills the sky.

Silly jokes sprout with each new burst,
A fruity chorus, oh, how it's cursed!
The trees shake gently, swaying to rhyme,
In this silly song, we've got the time!

Tune in close, you won't want to miss,
A fruity concert, such sweet bliss.
With every crunch, a pun awaits,
The laughter dances, it never abates!

So gather close, let's sing our song,
With every bite, you can't go wrong.
A symphony ripe, a chorus divine,
Join the fruit fest, let's all entwine!

Tasting Summer's Echo

A fruity orb in sunlit glow,
With skin like velvet, all aglow.
A taste of mischief, sweet and bright,
Squirrels plotting in delight.

Lemonade laughs, a splash, a cheer,
While bees dance close, we have no fear.
One juicy bite, a giggle's sound,
In summer's grip, we all are bound.

Adventures drip from every slice,
Fruit salad dreams feel oh-so-nice.
Sticky fingers, a race, a chase,
Caught in laughter, time can't erase.

Echoes linger, joyous delight,
In fleeting moments, we ignite.
With every taste, let smiles unfurl,
Summer's echo spins in a whirl.

Enchanted Harvests

In orchards wide, where laughter spills,
We sneak a bite, ignore the frills.
Barefoot wander, oh what a scene,
Our sticky toes in grass, so green!

A basket full, but can't resist,
A munch, a crunch, a fruity twist.
Giggles pop like bubbles of air,
These stolen treats, beyond compare.

The golden hour calls us near,
We swing on branches, full of cheer.
With every nibble, stories grow,
Enchanted harvests, joy in tow.

Sweet flavors dance like sprites in flight,
Among the trees, the day feels right.
In each juicy bite, we find a spark,
An orchard's laughter in the dark.

Charmed by Nature

Round and round, we spin like tops,
Nature offers us her chops.
A little hop, a fruity cheer,
The sun shines bright, our hearts feel clear.

Silly faces, laughter shared,
In sticky chaos, we are ensnared.
The tastiest treasure, full of glee,
Charmed by nature, wild and free.

With every bite, a silly dance,
Squirrels giggle, we take a chance.
Spinning tales of fruit so grand,
In this madness, hand in hand.

Nature's pranksters, bold and loud,
Amid the greens, we feel so proud.
Together we embrace the fun,
As nature laughs, we've just begun.

Tales of the Orchard

In an orchard where the laughter grows,
Tales of adventures dance like prose.
Each fruity legend, a burst of fun,
Chasing shadows in the midday sun.

Once a squirrel wore a berry hat,
He wobbled and giggled, just like that!
With each brave bite, he took the lead,
An acorn toast, his naughty creed.

Juicy whispers float through the air,
In every nook, mischief to share.
Fruit stains on shirts, stories unfold,
As roots weave tales both brave and bold.

From sticky fingers to grins so wide,
In this orchard, we all reside.
Mirthful magic, so bright and clear,
Telling tales of joy with cheer!

Violet Velvet Dreams

In gardens where the purple reigns,
The fruit hangs low, defying pains.
With every bite, a giggle bursts,
Oh, the joy of juicy firsts!

The squirrels plot with sneaky grins,
While ants march in their tiny bins.
Each squish, a soft and silly sound,
Echoes of laughter all around.

The juice flows freely, sticky bliss,
A sweet embrace you can't dismiss.
With friends, we gather, hats askew,
To snack on dreams of violet hue.

So raise a toast with fruit in hand,
To velvet dreams that we've all planned.
For life, like fruit, is full of cheer,
A funny burst we hold so dear.

A Dance of Tender Promises

Underneath the leafy shade,
Little fruits in bright parades.
They sway and spin with every breeze,
Whispering secrets among the trees.

With each step, a juicy plop,
We giggle loud and never stop.
Their laughter echoes in the air,
As we twirl 'round without a care.

The sun shines down, a golden crown,
On tender fruits in purple gowns.
With every bite, a story told,
Of happy dances, brave and bold.

So grab a friend and join the fun,
In this strange dance beneath the sun.
For life's a jig of fruity bliss,
With every crunch, a silly kiss.

Bursting with Joy

A basket filled with shiny gems,
They dance like tiny diadems.
Each munch a burst of laughter loud,
Beneath the shade, we're feeling proud.

They wobble on their stems so tight,
As if they're waiting for a bite.
With every squish, a gooey cheer,
Echoes of joy, so crystal clear.

The juice runs down, a sugary stream,
We laugh and slip; it's quite the theme.
In sticky hands, we make a pact,
To share the joy, and that's a fact.

So here we are, a merry crew,
With fruity wonders, bright and new.
Each bursting treat, a tale we share,
Of silly moments caught mid-air.

Luscious Sorrows

In gardens lush, the heartache grows,
Of perfect fruits that everyone knows.
We trip and tumble on the grass,
As juicy dreams come running past.

With every taste, a laugh or two,
For life is rich, but so is goo.
The sticky mess becomes our crown,
As luscious sorrows weigh us down.

With friends around, we drop the frown,
And wear our joy like a silly gown.
Each plump delight, a bittersweet,
For laughter hides beneath the beat.

So let's embrace this fruity plight,
With giggles bouncing, hearts so light.
For sorrow's just a funny game,
In gardens where we share the fame.

Sunkissed Desires

Sunkissed dreams on a tree,
Juicy giggles flowing free.
Birds are chirping a sweet tune,
Beneath the bright afternoon.

Sticky fingers and bright smiles,
Fruits that make you walk in styles.
Trying not to stain your shirt,
With every juicy, luscious squirt.

In the shade, we dance and play,
As fruits hanging invite our sway.
Laughing as they drop with grace,
Each one gifted, a joyful chase.

Tasting sweetness on a dare,
Messy faces everywhere.
With every bite, a burst of cheer,
Sunkissed wishes, summer's dear.

Essence of Eden

Here in Eden, laughter spills,
Fruits adorn with joyful thrills.
Rolling down the grassy slope,
Wishing for more than just hope.

Count the splashes, fruit fights bloom,
Sticky joy in every room.
Splat! A fruit flies through the air,
Landing right on someone's hair!

Sipping nectar, sweet delight,
Fruity dreams keep us up at night.
Chasing flavors, a daring quest,
In this paradise, we feel blessed.

Underneath the sunlit glow,
Mischief dances, spirits flow.
The essence here, a merry song,
In Eden's laughs, we all belong.

Between Blossom and Fruit

In springtime, blossoms paint the scene,
Tiny buds where laughter's keen.
A dance of petals in the breeze,
Tickled by the buzzing bees.

Just a step, and then we dash,
Fruits appear in a colorful splash.
Chasing colors, running wild,
Nature's canvas, a playful child.

Between the bloom and fruiting time,
We sip on joy, and sip on rhyme.
Fruits like jewels, a rainbow's feast,
With every bite, we're tamed at least.

Sprinkling laughter in the sun,
Among the branches, we all run.
Where blossoms dance and fruits will roll,
Life's a joke that fills the soul.

Purple Hues of Bliss

In fields of purple, giggles bloom,
Light and laughter fill the room.
Chasing shadows, here we play,
With purple treasures on display.

We taste the sweetness in the air,
A competition — who can dare?
To eat a fruit and not be stained,\nWith purple juice that leaves us drained!

Rolling laughter on the ground,
Purple joy is all around.
With every bite, our faces gleam,
Living life in a fruity dream.

Whimsical hues ignite our day,
In every bite, we laugh and sway.
Living fully, bliss we chase,
In shades of purple, we find our place.

A Symphony of Juices

In the bowl, they dance and sway,
Chubby fruits in bright array.
One took a dive, a fruity splat,
Now I'm stuck in this sticky mat!

Nature's snack, so sweetly round,
With every bite, joy's always found.
I wear a smear of purple hue,
A fashion choice, it's all the clue!

Give me a bread, I'll make it spread,
Smugly oozing, enough said!
A sandwich built with jam so bold,
Who knew a fruit could make me told?

So here we are, in fruit delight,
Juicy moments, they take flight.
Each sticky bite a playful jest,
Life's little quirks are truly best!

Beneath the Glistening Skin

Oh, the glimmer and the shine,
This fruit is truly divine.
I took a slice, it stared at me,
With its cheeky, juicy glee!

Beneath the skin, there lies a tale,
Of many bites, both sweet and pale.
A game of life, I munch away,
This berry's charm is here to stay!

It rolls away, a cheeky stunt,
I chase it down, no time to hunt.
A fruit that plays, it knows the score,
Each moment spent, I laugh and roar!

Such flavors burst, a comedy,
With every bite, absurdity.
I'm captured by this fruity grin,
So here's to laughter, let's dig in!

Dreams of a Fruitful Radiance

In visions made of sunny dreams,
Where laughter flows in fruity streams.
I see a feast of color bright,
A joyous splash, a pure delight!

They tumble down, a splendid sight,
Each globel round, a playful bite.
With giggles heard from every stone,
This joyous fruit is all my own!

To savor life, a bold embrace,
With sticky hands, it's quite the chase.
Juicy poets with fruit in hand,
We laugh together, oh so grand!

With every squeeze, a joyful shout,
In fruity peril, there's no doubt.
So raise a glass to fruit's delight,
Let's make it merry, every bite!

The Lure of Ruby Richness

See the colors, deep and bright,
A ruby world, what sheer delight!
I tried to eat it, slipped and flew,
A joyful mess, that much is true!

With every squish, I laugh in vain,
This fruit's a game, it's quite insane.
It rolls away, a clever tease,
How can this sweet be such a breeze?

Sticky fingers, face aglow,
Each nibble brings a funny show.
A fruit that knows how to be fun,
Who knew delight could weigh a ton?

So here's to cheer, to juicy dreams,
In fruity mess where laughter beams.
Let's raise a glass, a toasty cheer,
For ruby treasures we hold dear!

Fleshy Crescendos

In orchards where the laughter sways,
The fruit hangs low in sunny rays.
A plop, a squish, a juicy splash,
We dive right in, it's quite the bash.

With every bite, a giggle bursts,
Sticky hands, oh how it thirsts.
Our faces painted, a colorful spree,
Who thought fruit could be so carefree?

We roll and tumble on the ground,
In fruity chaos, joy is found.
A chorus of squeals, a vibrant sight,
Nature's jest, a pure delight.

So grab a basket, let's take flight,
To nibble, munch, from day to night.
In this whimsical dance, we sway,
Join in the fun, come out and play!

Radiant Abundance

A bounty bright, they roll and gleam,
In heaps of trouble, we all scream.
A picnic spread on checkered cloth,
A feast of giggles, oh, what a froth!

Round and round, like bowling balls,
We launch them high, they take the falls.
With every smash, the laughter grows,
Who knew such joy from little prose?

Banana peels can't hold a flame,
To fruity antics, we're always game.
The fruit brigade, our happy crew,
Join our revelry, it's fun for two!

So let's embrace this fruity flare,
With every squish, have not a care.
Life's a riot, in flavors bold,
Chase the giggles, let joys unfold!

Sweet Shadows

In twilight's glow, we dance and play,
A slice of fun in fading day.
Sweetness drips, as laughter rolls,
In joyous mirth, we lose our souls.

Among the trees, a game we weave,
With secret paths, we never leave.
Shadow puppets in fruit delight,
Silly faces in the night.

The fruit brigade, with giggles loud,
Make fruity friends, we feel so proud.
Whirling round like wild balloons,
Underneath the silver moons.

Grab a friend for this delight,
Fruity mischief, purest sight.
In shadows deep, let's carve a mark,
Of sweetened chaos, fun's own spark!

Juicy Journeys

We packed our bags with fruit supreme,
On a road trip, life's sweetest dream.
Bumpy rides lead to juicy finds,
With every pit-stop, laughter binds.

A fruit catapult? Let's give it a try,
Launching snacks into the sky.
Sticky fingers, and giggles ensue,
Who needs a map when joy's in view?

From peachy hills to berry fields,
The laughter flows as our joy yields.
In every bite, a silly cheer,
On this adventure, nothing to fear.

With every mile, the fun compiles,
Our juicy journey brings forth smiles.
So gather 'round, let stories flow,
In fruity warmth, our hearts will glow!

The Wild Orchard's Lullaby

In the orchard, fruits do sway,
They whisper jokes, come out to play.
With laughter ripe upon each branch,
The squirrels join in, a fruity dance.

Bees buzz around with a cheeky grin,
While birds are giggling, 'Let's begin!'
The apples blush, jealous and bright,
As cherries crack jokes through the night.

A pear slips down, whoops, what a fall!
The apples roar, 'Come join our ball!'
The moonlight shines on this silly spree,
Garnished by laughter from fruit and bee.

So let the harvest bring delight,
With every bite, a silly sight.
The wild orchard, with all its cheer,
Holds a lullaby for all who hear.

Midday Reverie

Under the sun, the fruits all sunbathe,
Spreading rumors, oh what a wraith!
'Did you see the peach's strange dance?'
While berries giggle, caught in a trance.

The apples boast of their shiny skin,
While pears laugh loud, 'Oh where to begin?'
A wandering breeze, it brings a tease,
'Who's plumper today? Let's have a squeeze!'

A fig pops up, 'I'm here too, you know!'
The grapes all shush, 'Oh, take it slow!'
In the midday sun, the fruits play their game,
With friends all around, they feel no shame.

Laughter echoes through vine and tree,
In this dreamy realm, oh so carefree.
Each fruit declared it's the silliest round,
In midday reverie, joy's always found.

Harvest Moon Serenade

Under the harvest moon's bright glow,
Fruits gather 'round, putting on a show.
'Twas my turn to shine,' the cherries proclaim,
While the oranges claim 'We're all the same!'

The night is alive with their playful tunes,
As shadows dance beneath silver moons.
'An apple a day keeps the humor alive!'
This jovial gang, they start to thrive.

With laughter echoing through the night,
The berries prepare a pie for a bite.
As bowls of fun are spread wide and far,
Each fruit a star, no matter who they are.

So raise a toast to the fruits of the night,
Their dance beneath the moon is a glorious sight.
In this serenade of silliness and cheer,
The harvest moon brightens the atmosphere.

Winesap Confessions

In a corner where the winesaps dwell,
They swap tales and giggle as well.
'Did you hear about the pear's big crush?'
The whispers spread, causing quite a rush.

'Oh stop!' cries out the lossy old grape,
'You think you're the star? You're all an escape!'
But the apples just cackle, 'Look who's in line!'
It's the prune who sings, 'Oh, I feel divine!'

With secrets spilled among the drink,
Each fruit brims with laughter, we all need a wink.
The room fills with mirth, oh what a delight,
In this fruity confessional, all's out tonight.

So gather around for a chat in the dark,
Where jokes are sweet and laughter's the spark.
For in the heart of this fruit-filled spree,
Winesap confessions speak truthfully!

Ripe Sunlit Spheres

Round and shiny, they gleam so bright,
A fruit parade, what a funny sight!
Dancing in baskets, in rows they stand,
Smirking at apples, like they own the land.

Their laughter echoes, a juicy jest,
"Bet you can't guess who's the sweetest guest?"
With a wink and a nod, they poke and tease,
Adventurous spirits swaying in the breeze.

Fruits of delight in a sunlit cheer,
Rolling down hills, oh how we cheer!
A bounce and a roll, a game of tag,
The berries just giggle, and the grapes all brag.

When summertime comes, they take the stage,
Giggling giggles, younger than age.
Ripe and ready for a feast to start,
These sunlit spheres sure know how to part!

The Sweetness Within

Beneath the skin, there's magic play,
A burst of laughter in every way.
Shrunken grapes look on with envy wide,
As luscious giggles kidnap their pride.

The moment you bite, a joke is revealed,
Sour faces fade, congratulations sealed.
"Who's laughing now?" the sweetness calls,
While citrus fruit simply twirls and falls.

They waltz in bowls, with a cheeky flair,
Twirling in circles without a care.
Luring in kids with sugary charms,
"Come taste our bliss, we'll sound the alarms!"

So bite, oh friend, don't hold back the fun,
Join in the laughter, let joy be spun.
The sweetness within is pure delight,
Under the stars, we party all night!

Nectar of the Orchard

In a dreamy orchard, laughter flows,
Where juicy treasures share their prose.
Bumbling bees with their sticky tales,
Flaunt their buzz like tiny pails.

The nectar drips with a giggling sound,
While squirrels hold court in their royal mound.
"Join the feast, don't be shy!" they yell,
As sticky fingers cast their spell.

Rolling in sunlight, like kids at play,
The fruits share secrets in a merry way.
Twisting and turning, a fruity ballet,
They tickle the senses and brighten the day.

So toast to the orchard, and raise your cup,
To nectar and laughter, let's drink it up!
Gather your friends, let the fun begin,
In the heart of the orchard, let smiles win!

Juicy Embrace of Summer

Warmth wraps around in a juicy embrace,
As laughter bounces, filling the space.
Fruits in the sun, they strike a pose,
Sporting their bikinis, just look at those!

Hilarious antics as they prance around,
Juicy jokes waiting to astound.
Grapes vie for the crown, and cherries wet,
"Next summer you'll see, bet on our bet!"

Watermelon sings, "I'm the king of this day!"
As mint leaves giggle, "Just taste my sway!"
Bananas flip-flop, with a cheerful shout,
"Let's split this party and kick it about!"

Endless fun under the summer sun,
A juicy embrace, oh, let's all run!
With flavors a-dancing and laughter galore,
Let's savor together, who could ask for more?

Echoes of Late Summer

In the garden, a dance of sweet taste,
Fruits wobble as they race to find space.
They giggle and bounce, no care for the fall,
A jolly parade in the sun's golden sprawl.

The squirrels shake their heads in pure disbelief,
As the grapes boast about their new leaf.
"Who's juicier now? You or me?" they all shout,
With a chuckle so loud, the whole orchard's in doubt.

In the breeze, a soft whisper of jam,
Strawberries blushing, they're all part of the fam.
"Let's blend into smoothies!" they tease with a cheer,
While the apples stand still, clutching their fear.

As the sun sets low, the fun doesn't fade,
The fruits laugh together, their worries delayed.
In this garden of laughter, there's always a twist,
Where every fruit dreams of a moment, unmissed.

A Portrait of Juicy Delight

There's a cherry with shades, feeling quite bold,
Posing for selfies, their story unfolds.
"Look at my stem! Isn't it fine?" they preen,
While the others roll eyes, oh what a scene!

The watermelon feels like summer's big hit,
Spilling its seeds, not caring a bit.
"Let's have a picnic, no need to be shy,"
Calls out the mango, waving its goodbye.

Pineapples in hats, sipping on drinks,
Spreading their wisdom, now that's how it blinks!
"Life's more refreshing when we raise a glass,"
Bantering louder, they let the time pass.

But when evening falls, and the stars take their cue,
They gather 'round laughter, sharing their view.
In the orchard of joy, with flavors so rare,
Every fruit knows that it's best when we share.

Fruits of Indulgence

Peaches are plotting a scheme oh so sweet,
With a wink and a nod, they plan a retreat.
"The melons are bringing a party tonight,
Bring your vibes and your juice; it'll be quite a sight!"

The lingering mango has all of the flair,
"Just wait till you see my fancy new hair!"
While the limes zesty, sparkled in green,
Chime in with laughter, they're part of the scene.

The coconuts chimed in with plans for a splash,
A tropical twist, folks, it's bound to be rash!
So they roll on the grass, all sides in delight,
Giggling and wiggling until it's goodnight!

And as the moon glows, they give a loud cheer,
For each fruity companion who brings so much cheer.
In their fruity utopia, where laughter runs wild,
This colorful crew is forever a child.

Ripe Reverie

In the orchard today, the air is all jam,
With berries that bounce and a cheeky old lamb.
"Who knew that fruit could have such grand dreams?"
Whispers a peach, bursting out at the seams.

"Let's host a contest for the juiciest prize,
We'll shorten our pants to fit in our size!"
The oranges chuckle, their zest in a spin,
"Each drop that we spill is a victory grin!"

Bananas slip by with a giggle and glide,
"Watch out for humor, we're all on this ride!"
With each little laugh, the orchard feels light,
A miracle moment; everything's right.

So as dusk settles down, they dance to the plate,
With flavors and giggles, they're sealing their fate.
In this whimsical world, oh what a delight,
Where each fruit's a star, shining ever so bright!

Luscious Delights

Round and sweet, a little treat,
Juicy bites that can't be beat.
Wobbling softly on the tree,
Nature's candy, wild and free.

With every crush, a purple splash,
Sticky fingers, quite the mishmash.
Laughing loud as juices flow,
Wonders few can truly know.

When life gives you fruit in hand,
Make a joke, life's not so bland.
Squeeze the day, embrace the fun,
Who knew a fruit could weigh a ton?

So here's to life, a fruity chase,
In every bite, a silly face.
With luscious bites we dance and sing,
Who'd have thought such joy a fruit could bring?

Alluring Hues

In shades of purple, blush, and gold,
These fruity treasures dare be bold.
They wink and sparkle in the sun,
Each bite promises a ton of fun.

With skins so shiny, like a show,
A rainbow offering, row by row.
One tastes sweet, the other tart,
A fruity riddle for the heart.

The bait on trees, the eye's bright tease,
Nature's palette sure to please.
With every chew, a quirky grin,
Who knew fruit could make us spin?

Let's giggle at the taste parade,
In this fruity masquerade.
With laughter ripe, let's play this game,
Alluring hues, a tasty fame!

Nature's Gem

A treasure hangs upon the vine,
Glistening berries, oh so fine.
Roaming fields where laughter grows,
Sweet little gems in nature's throes.

They dangle low, they swing and sway,
Inviting all to come and play.
With every munch, the joy erupts,
Nature's candy factory, abrupts.

Who would think nature's little spheres,
Could fill our hearts with giggles and cheers?
A burst of sweetness in each bite,
A fruity puzzle, pure delight.

So grab a handful, don't be shy,
Taste the whimsy, wink and fly.
In every pluck, a story's spun,
Nature's gems are never done!

Juxtaposition of Flavor

In one corner, sugar's kiss,
In another, tartness, oh so bliss.
A chaotic dance on the tongue,
Where giggles are ripe, and joy is sung.

Mixing flavors, what a sight,
Every fruit a playful fight.
Sweet and sour, round and round,
In this brawl, joy is found.

With every burst, the world spins bright,
Funny faces, what a sight!
Snack time's here, the showdown's set,
With fruity laughter, no regret.

Thus we toast to each wild bite,
Juxtaposed flavors, pure delight.
Come join the fun, let's celebrate,
A fruity party on our plate!

The Warmth of Sunlit Days

In gardens bright, the fruit does sway,
A cheeky dance in sun's sweet ray.
With cheeks so round, they laugh and grin,
In juicy tales, the fun begins.

A sticky hand, a gleeful shout,
Chasing drops, we twist about.
In warm embrace, we spin and twirl,
With fruity joys, our hearts unfurl.

Each bite a burst, a zesty prank,
The laughter dances, giddy flank.
Upon the grass, we flop and roll,
Sweet sticky wonders fill our soul.

Petals on the Breeze

A rosy blush with laughter flies,
As winds play tricks, and fruit complies.
Slippery tales of a fruit parade,
Silly antics never fade.

Petals swirl like twirling tops,
We giggle hard till someone drops.
Fruity giggles in the air,
Oh, what a sight, what a fruity affair!

The trees chuckle, the bushes grin,
As we dive in, let the fun begin.
Who knew joy could taste this sweet?
In every bite, we find our beat.

Garden's Crown Jewel

In the garden's heart, a treasure gleams,
A humorous twist on fruity dreams.
With pouts and laughs, we seek and find,
The jewel of joy that's intertwined.

A bounty bright, so bold, and round,
With giggles high, as we run 'round.
Garden kings, we take our throne,
In fruity crowns, we're never alone.

Tickled by leaves, we leap and roll,
In fruity folly, we lose control.
The laughter rings beneath the sun,
In our garden, the fun's never done!

Fruity Harmonies

With melodies sung by buzzing bees,
Our fruity chorus floats on the breeze.
A symphony sweet that makes us sway,
In every bite, a bright cabaret.

Laughter and joy in every note,
A fruity jingle, we all emote.
The juice runs down, we waltz and spin,
As nature's jesters, we laugh and grin.

Each flavor a song, each texture a tune,
We dance together beneath the moon.
In our fruity fest, the world feels right,
With each silly bite, we take flight.

Taste of the Sun

Under bright skies, they hang so low,
A juicy treasure, a sweetened glow.
Birds eye the bounty, think it's a feast,
But they're dining on snacks, like it or least!

With each little bite, summer's on parade,
Giggles erupt as sticky hands invade.
The juice runs freely, a messy delight,
We laugh and we slurp, until it feels right!

A tart little wink, and a sweet little cheer,
The taste of the sun, it brings everyone near.
With laughter and friends, we savor the fun,
Oh, the joy of the fruit, oh, how we run!

In every small bite, there's pure jubilation,
A festival of flavors, a joyful creation.
So grab one or two, let the giggles take flight,
In the garden of sun, everything feels right!

Hidden in the Canopy

In a green world where secrets sleep,
Fruits hide away in a bough so deep.
I search for a snack, all hopeful and bright,
And find myself snagged on a branch in mid-flight!

A treasure I spy, nestled in shade,
The fruit of my dreams, oh, the risk I've made.
I reach with my hand, a daring display,
Then tumble right down in a fruity ballet!

Between dappled leaves, there's joy all around,
With laughter erupting, I stumble and bound.
A vibrant sphere, so round and so sweet,
Tastes better with laughter—oh, what a treat!

So here in the canopy, I'll make my stand,
With silly apologies to all that I planned.
Hidden no more, I'll shout out with glee,
For fun's in the hunt for what's high on the tree!

The Flavor of Farewell

In a basket of dreams, I gather them tight,
The flavors of summer, a glorious sight.
But here comes the autumn, with chilly goodbyes,
As fruit slips away, oh, how the heart sighs!

On the last sunny day, let's savor the thrill,
A taste of nostalgia, a sweet little chill.
We feast on the bounty, as laughter takes flight,
Extracting each drop in the warm waning light!

With every last bite, it's a flavorful fight,
Against memories fading as day turns to night.
But cheers to the moments, let's drink up the cheer,
For each fruity farewell brings joy year to year!

So I'll raise a toast to the flavors we've known,
To the laughter and sunshine, our hearts will have grown.
With giggles, we part, yet it's not really done,
For inside of our hearts, still tastes of the sun!

The Dance of Ripening

In twilight's embrace, they begin to sway,
Fruits wobble and jiggle, a fruity ballet.
They twirl with the breeze, under stars shining bright,
A dance of temptation, oh, what a sight!

In their vibrant gowns, they prance with delight,
Every bump and each wiggle feels just right.
Oh, the fun of   ripening! What a show,
I join in the dance, with a big, silly glow!

The laughter erupts, as we all join the scene,
With juicy spontaneity, we shimmy and glean.
Through sunlight and moonlight, we mix and we sway,
As the fruits put on performances, day after day!

So raise up your glasses to the dance on the vine,
Where friendship and laughter combine so divine.
Let's cap off this jig with a delectable bite,
For when fruits come to play, everything feels right!

Rich Fields of Promise

In fields of green and purple hues,
Chasing butterflies, I sang the blues.
With plump delights that danced on skin,
I cracked a joke, let the munching begin!

A farmer shouted, 'Watch that tree!'
I laughed so hard, I tripped on glee.
A tumble here, a rhyme, a roll,
These fruits of joy, they fill my soul!

With every bite, a chuckle spills,
Sweet juice and laughter give me thrills.
The fruits do jig and juggle, too,
Oh, what a sight for folks like you!

So gather 'round, let's feast today,
These berries have come out to play.
With every tart, a pun shall rise,
Laughter's the treat, oh what a prize!

Nature's Profound Lyric

In nature's book, each page a fruit,
A clever quip, a funny pursuit.
The garden sings, so sweet and spry,
Beneath the sun, we laugh and pry.

A squirrel danced, thought he could steal,
But I outsmarted him with a meal!
'No nuts today,' I said with glee,
The fruits of joy belong to me!

With every gust, the branches sway,
The fruits giggle in a playful way.
It's quite a sight, this fruity tease,
Nature's gift, meant to appease!

So let us rhyme, and let us munch,
On silly thoughts, a hearty bunch.
With all this mirth, the world's a stage,
We're the jesters, the fruits our wage!

Pathways of Flavor

In gardens wide, I took a stroll,
A path of flavor, pure as gold.
Each fruit a gem, each laugh a cheer,
Together here, we have no fear!

With every twist and turn, I grin,
A fruity road, let the jokes begin.
Oh, what a trip, so sweet and bright,
Nature's path, a pure delight!

Berry bushes hum a tune,
Underneath the grinning moon.
Each step I take, my heart does race,
In this fruity, funny place!

So gather friends, don't be too shy,
Let's nibble clouds and laugh up high.
On these pathways paved with fun,
We'll eat and laugh until we run!

The Song of the Orchard

In orchards wide, the fruits do sing,
A mighty tune, oh what a fling!
With raucous laughter, let it ring,
Each bite, a joy, a wonderful thing!

A crow tries to join the fun-filled fray,
But trips on words, oh what a display!
He caws and hoots, but can't catch a tune,
While we munch on berries, 'neath the silly moon!

The blossoms dance, the squirrels prance,
While we sit back, entranced by chance.
With every crunch, a jest does sprout,
This song of laughter, we can't live without!

So here's to orchards, rich and bright,
Where apples and giggles share the night.
Let's join the chorus, loud and clear,
In the orchard's laugh, there's nothing to fear!

The Sweetest Temptation

In the orchard, I spy a treat,
Round and glossy, oh so neat.
A bite so juicy, it makes me grin,
Dripping sweetness, where do I begin?

With every nibble, joy takes flight,
My sticky fingers, a comical sight.
Friends around share in my delight,
Laughing out loud, what a silly bite!

The bees are buzzing, what a scene,
Chasing me like I'm a sweet routine.
I bolt and dash, can't let them win,
But oh this fruit, it draws me in!

So here's the secret, let's not pretend,
This delectable treasure, it's hard to defend.
With giggles and glee, I'll take my chance,
For who can resist such a fruity dance?

Essence of Dusk

As daylight fades, a funny sight,
Fruits glow softly in evening light.
I grab one quick, but it's a trick,
It jumps right out, oh what a flick!

With laughter ringing, I chase around,
This sneaky fruit won't be found.
It dodges my grasp, oh so sly,
Tickling my toes as it rolls by.

Underneath the twilight, I break into cheer,
For the sprightliest fruit is finally near.
With a leap and a giggle, I make my stand,
This fruity chase, it's planned and unplanned!

As shadows deepen, I claim my prize,
Juicy delight under starry skies.
With friends nearby, we dance and laugh,
In the sweetness of dusk, we'll relish each gaffe!

Silken Fruits

In the summer sun, so bright and clear,
Silken fruits are bringing cheer.
With every bite so smooth and round,
Laughter erupts with every sound.

I tried to juggle, what a feat!
One slipped away, oh what a treat!
It rolled across the grass so green,
And landed right where I'd never seen!

Splat! It hit my buddy's shoe,
Now sticky toes, who knew it too?
With giggling fits, we share the blame,
In this fruity game, it's all the same!

So we dive in, with chuckles loud,
Making a mess, we are so proud.
Beneath the sun's soft, golden glow,
Fruity fun is the way to go!

The Orchard's Embrace

In the orchard's arm, we gather near,
With fruits so plump, we've nothing to fear.
A friendly competition, who can eat fast?
With laughter and joy, we've made a blast!

As each fruit vanishes, so do our woes,
A feast of giggles, the best one goes!
Sticky hands and silly faces,
We embrace the mess, no need for graces.

Watch out for the seeds, they take flight,
Catapulting laughter into the night.
With every toss, our spirits soar,
Competing for the best, who could ask for more?

So let's raise a cheer, for nature's prank,
In this orchard hug, we all can tank.
With joy in abundance, we gleefully chase,
The sweetest moments, in this special place!

A Tribute to August's Bounty

Oh, summer's treat in a tiny sphere,
Juicy delight that draws us near.
With every bite, a giggle spills,
Nature's candy, it triggers thrills.

Dripped juice stains on our shirts so bold,
Sticky fingers as we're told,
To eat with joy, no forks required,
These treasures, they are much desired.

Under the sun, we dance around,
For laughter blooms where joy is found.
Who knew fruit could bring such cheer?
With each squished bite, we shed a tear!

So here's to the month that makes us grin,
A round of fruit to tuck our chins in.
Let's toast to harvests, let's celebrate,
For these juicy gems are truly great!

Cascading Flavor

Round and plump with a cheeky smile,
They roll and bounce, oh what a while!
Sweet and tangy in every part,
Squeezed into jam, they steal our heart.

With a crunch and squirt, oh what a mess,
Sticky hands lead to full-on finesse.
Why wear a bib? That's just plain lame,
We take our chances, it's all a game.

The juice runs wild, like a silly stream,
Creating moments, together we beam.
In pie or tart, or just on their own,
These tiny delights are zestfully known.

Flavor cascades, it bursts and swirls,
An explosion of joy, oh how it twirls!
Join the fun, take a big bite,
For laughter and sweetness dance in the night!

Shadows of the Branch

Underneath the tree, we gather near,
Shadows dancing, laughter clear.
Red and purple, a colorful sight,
Picking the fruit feels just right.

Squeezing tight with giggling pleas,
The juice runs free on summer's breeze.
With each new bite, we can't help but play,
The shadows of branches sway and sway.

Splatters and dribbles, sticky feet,
Oh what fun, this fruity treat!
As friends they dangle, a jolly bunch,
We munch and laugh, oh what a crunch!

A treasure found in the midst of trees,
Stained fingers and laughter, such sweet memories.
Raise a cheer for nature's fine prank,
In the shade of the branches, we fill our tank!

In the Shade of Sweetness

In warm sun rays, we lie in wait,
To feast on fruits that truly rate.
A game of flavor, hit or miss,
With every bite, we seal our bliss.

They roll like laughter across the ground,
Orange and purple, they spin around.
Squished in pockets, oh what a sight,
Sticky treasures that bring delight.

Under the branches, we play our part,
Creating chaos, it's a candy art!
Falling laughter fills the air,
Sweetness found in daydreams rare.

So here's to bites of character bold,
Wrapped in laughter, the stories told.
In the shade, with joy in our hearts,
Every juicy moment, where fun never departs!

Vibrant Harvest

A fruit so round, it winks at me,
Hiding in leaves, a cheeky spree.
I pinch it gently, it gives a grin,
A juicy trickster, let the fun begin!

Neighbors sniff, they claim it's grand,
But in my hand, it's comically planned.
With every bite, a squirt, oh dear!
I wear my treasure, sticky with cheer!

Each basket's filled with purple clowns,
Once regal trees now dance in gowns.
They giggle low, whispering tales,
About their heists and fruity scales!

Slicing, dicing, juice up to my ears,
It's a fruity party, laugh through the years.
With sugary coats and puns so spry,
Fruit salad giggles, oh me, oh my!

Tales of the Bursting Fruit

Once in the orchard, quite a sight,
A fruit fell down; it took off in flight!
Bouncing around, it's quite absurd,
"Catch me if you can!" the ripe one stirred.

The farmer chased, his hat askew,
While laughter echoed, as if on cue.
Every turn a squishy surprise,
Near madcap antics, oh how it flies!

Bubbly laughter from each tight space,
Who knew a fruit could win a race?
Bursting joy, oh what a show,
This rebel round, put on a glow!

Jars of jam that went astray,
Fruit lovers grinned in wild dismay.
They'd shriek and giggle at the daring cheer,
Best fruit tales for everyone near!

Ecstasy of the Earth

In gardens green, the mischief brews,
Fruits exchange jokes over morning dues.
Wobbly rows of glee do sway,
While butterflies join this fun ballet!

Cheeky roots tickle the sun,
Making sure the laughter's spun.
With whispers sweet beneath each leaf,
"Consider us the best of beef!"

The earth hums back, a chuckle loud,
As insects groove, they form a crowd.
Each buried seed sharing its plight,
"Who knew we could bring such delight?"

So let us toast to silly times,
With nature's giggles and rhyming chimes.
An orchard's joy, forever free,
In earthy fun, we find our glee!

The Luscious Unraveling

A treasure sits, so round and bold,
It blushes deep, a story told.
I dared to snack, it burst and squirted,
My tee shirt's now the one that's hurted!

Among the vines, a playtime waits,
Bunches giggle, flaunting their plates.
A fruit parade in laughter's spree,
Join the carnival, come dance with me!

One slice gets jealous, starts a fight,
"Why can't I be the favorite bite?"
So juicy antics fill the air,
With fruity friends, we have not a care!

Finally, a feast, it's all in fun,
Laughter drips like that sticky run.
So raise a toast to the crazy fruit,
For every chuckle, it's truly a hoot!

Shades of Serenity

In the orchard, colors collide,
Round and juicy, they take pride.
Dancing squirrels play a game,
Fruits are laughing, it's all the same.

Sun-kissed cheeks in twisty trees,
Giggles float upon the breeze.
Bouncing balls of zingy cheer,
Who knew fruit could bring such beer?

A Bite of Bliss

Oh, what joy, a fruit so sweet,
Nibble here, it's quite the treat.
Juices dribble, spill with glee,
Oops! My shirt, oh woe is me!

Friends all gather, laughter blooms,
As sticky fingers fill the room.
One rogue bite, a splat and mess,
Yet tasty bites just bring success.

Harvest Moon Delight

Underneath the harvest moon,
Fruits are giggling, oh so soon.
Blushing bright in silver light,
They whisper secrets, taking flight.

Ripe and ready, on they sway,
Like a dance party in the hay.
With every chomp, the stars do wink,
Oh! What fun, we'll never think!

Velvet Skins

With velvet skins that gleam and glow,
These little jokers put on a show.
I take a bite, a grand surprise,
Juicy laughs from open skies.

Plucking one, I miss, oh dear!
Bouncing back, it rolls right here.
Laughter bubbles, it's quite absurd,
From fruit to fool, the line's blurred.